MECHANICAL VENTILATION

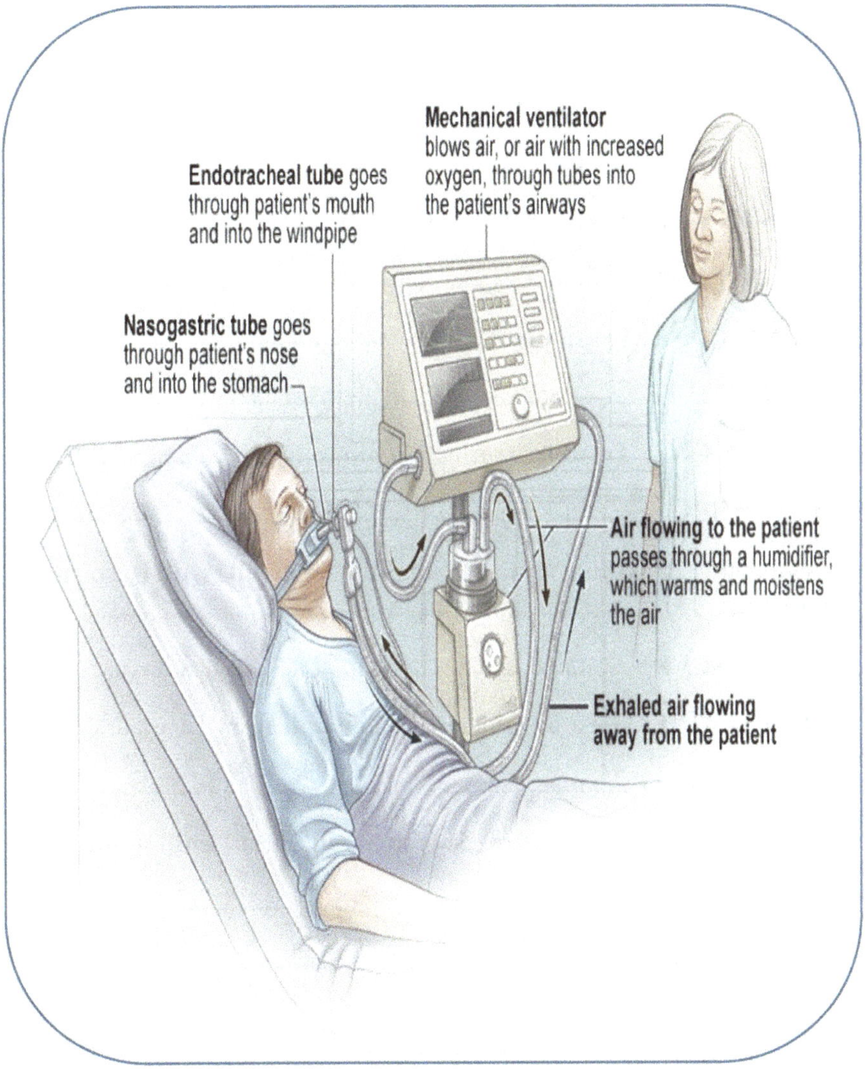

AF408391

TABLE OF CONTENTS

COURSE OVERVIEW

This comprehensive course is designed to provide healthcare providers with an in-depth understanding of mechanical ventilation, from fundamental principles to advanced applications and emerging technologies. The course covers the physiology of mechanical ventilation, different ventilatory modes and settings, monitoring and assessment strategies, troubleshooting common issues, and providing optimal support to patients with respiratory failure. Additionally, it explores cutting-edge advancements in mechanical ventilation, including precision ventilation, telemedicine, and regenerative therapies.

COURSE OBJECTIVES

By the end of this course, participants will be able to Understand the Fundamentals of Mechanical Ventilation, Master Different Ventilatory Modes and Settings, Monitor and Assess Ventilated Patients, Troubleshoot Common Ventilatory Issues, Provide Optimal Support to Patients with Respiratory Failure, Explore Advanced Topics and Emerging Technologies, Integrate Evidence-Based Practices into Clinical Care. By achieving these objectives, participants will be equipped with the knowledge and skills to excel in the management of mechanically ventilated patients, ultimately contributing to better health outcomes and improved quality of care.

COURSE MATERIALS

To learn this course, **healthcare providers/ participants** must be provided with materials like a Pen, pencil, notebook, and notepad to better understand and make it easy for them to learn.

INTRODUCTION

Mechanical ventilation is a critical component in the management of patients with respiratory failure and other severe respiratory conditions. It is a lifesaving intervention that healthcare providers must thoroughly understand to ensure optimal patient outcomes. This book, "Mastering Mechanical Ventilation: A Comprehensive Guide for Healthcare Providers," is designed to equip healthcare professionals with the knowledge and skills necessary to effectively use mechanical ventilators in clinical practice.

This book aims to provide a comprehensive understanding of mechanical ventilation, from the basic principles to advanced strategies. It covers the different modes of ventilation, ventilator settings, troubleshooting common issues, and how to provide optimal support to patients. Whether you are a novice just starting in the field or an experienced practitioner looking to deepen your knowledge, this book offers valuable insights and practical guidance.

Mechanical ventilation can be complex, with various modes and settings that must be tailored to each patient's needs. Understanding the physiological principles underlying mechanical ventilation is crucial for making informed decisions. This book begins by introducing the fundamental concepts and principles that form the foundation of mechanical ventilation. We then delve into the different modes of ventilation, exploring their indications, advantages, and limitations.

<h1 align="center">MODULE ONE</h1>

<h2 align="center">LESSON ONE: MECHANICAL VENTILATION</h2>

Mechanical ventilation is an essential intervention for patients who are unable to maintain adequate

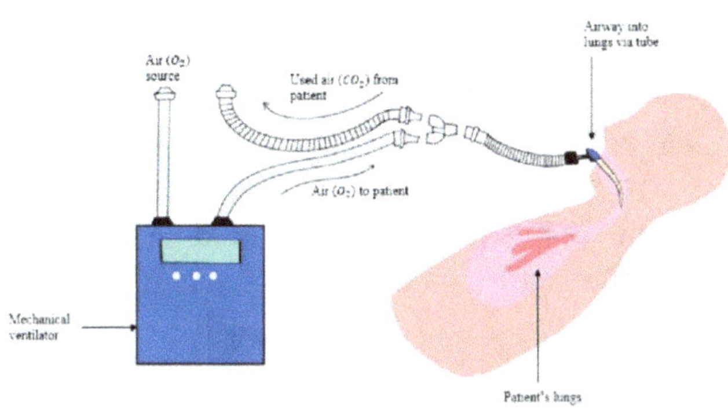

ventilation and oxygenation on their own. It is commonly used in critical care settings, such as intensive care units (ICUs), emergency departments, and surgeries requiring general anaesthesia.

History of Mechanical Ventilation

The history of mechanical ventilation dates back to the early 20th century. The first mechanical ventilators were manually operated devices used to provide positive pressure ventilation during anaesthesia. Over the years, significant advancements have been made in the design and functionality of mechanical ventilators, transforming them into sophisticated machines capable of providing precise and customizable respiratory support.

Indications for Mechanical Ventilation

Mechanical ventilation is indicated in various clinical scenarios, including:

- **Acute respiratory failure:** This condition occurs when the lungs cannot provide sufficient oxygen to the blood or remove carbon dioxide from the body. It can result from various causes, such as severe pneumonia, acute respiratory distress syndrome (ARDS), chronic obstructive pulmonary disease (COPD) exacerbations, and neuromuscular disorders.

- **Hypoxemic respiratory failure:** Characterized by low oxygen levels in the blood, this type of respiratory failure often requires mechanical ventilation to improve oxygenation.
- **Hypercapnic respiratory failure:** In this condition, elevated carbon dioxide levels in the blood necessitate mechanical ventilation to remove excess carbon dioxide and correct respiratory acidosis.
- **Apnea:** Patients who experience periods of apnea or temporary cessation of breathing may require mechanical ventilation to maintain adequate ventilation and prevent hypoxia.
- **Surgical procedures:** Mechanical ventilation is routinely used during surgeries requiring general anaesthesia to ensure proper ventilation and oxygenation.

Basic Concepts of Mechanical Ventilation

Mechanical ventilation involves the use of a machine known as a ventilator to assist or replace spontaneous breathing. The ventilator delivers a controlled flow of gas into the patient's lungs, either through a mask (non-invasive ventilation) or an endotracheal tube (invasive ventilation). The primary goals of mechanical ventilation are to:

- Ensure adequate oxygenation and ventilation
- Reduce the work of breathing
- Maintain airway patency
- Prevent ventilator-induced lung injury

Components of a Mechanical Ventilator

A mechanical ventilator consists of several key components, including:

Gas delivery system: This system delivers a mixture of oxygen and air to the patient. The gas is typically humidified and warmed to body temperature to prevent airway irritation.

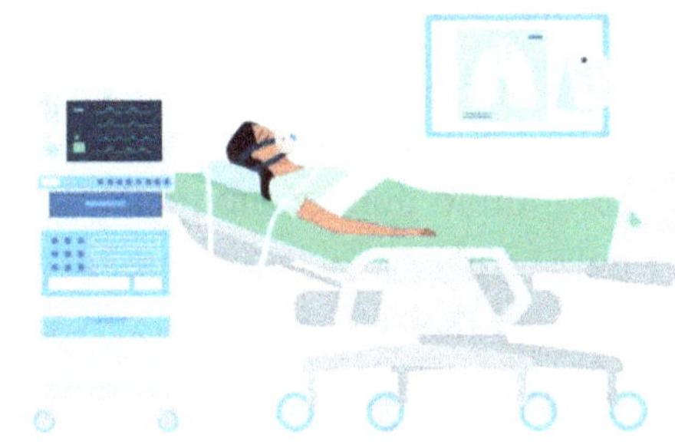

- **Control system:** The control system regulates the delivery of gas based on preset parameters, such as tidal volume, respiratory rate, and inspiratory pressure.
- **Monitoring system:** Ventilators are equipped with monitors that provide real-time data on various parameters, including airway pressure, tidal volume, and oxygen saturation. These monitors help healthcare providers assess the patient's respiratory status and adjust settings as needed.
- **Alarms:** Ventilators have built-in alarms to alert healthcare providers to potential issues, such as high or low airway pressures, disconnections, or apnea.

Ventilator Settings

Mechanical ventilators allow healthcare providers to adjust various settings to tailor ventilation to the patient's needs. Key ventilator settings include:

- Tidal volume (VT): The volume of air delivered to the lungs with each breath. It is typically set based on the patient's ideal body weight to prevent lung overdistension.
- Respiratory rate (RR): The number of breaths delivered per minute. This setting can be adjusted to maintain appropriate levels of oxygen and carbon dioxide in the blood.

- Positive end-expiratory pressure (PEEP): The pressure maintained in the lungs at the end of exhalation to keep the alveoli open and improve oxygenation.
- Inspiratory pressure (IP): The pressure applied during inspiration to deliver the tidal volume.
- Fraction of inspired oxygen (FiO2): The concentration of oxygen in the gas mixture delivered to the patient. FiO2 can be adjusted to maintain adequate oxygenation while minimizing the risk of oxygen toxicity.

Types of Mechanical Ventilation

There are two primary types of mechanical ventilation:

1. **Invasive ventilation:** Invasive ventilation involves the insertion of an endotracheal tube or tracheostomy tube into the patient's airway to deliver breaths directly to the lungs. It is commonly used in patients with severe respiratory failure or during surgeries requiring general anesthesia.
2. **Non-invasive ventilation:** Non-invasive ventilation (NIV) delivers breaths through a mask that covers the nose, mouth, or both. It is often used in patients with less severe respiratory failure or those who require temporary respiratory support.

DISCUSSION QUESTIONS

- What are the key differences between volume-controlled ventilation (VCV) and pressure-controlled ventilation (PCV), and in what clinical scenarios might each be preferred?
- How do changes in compliance and resistance affect the settings and performance of a mechanical ventilator? Discuss with examples of specific respiratory conditions.

MODULE TWO

LESSON ONE: PRINCIPLES OF MECHANICAL VENTILATION

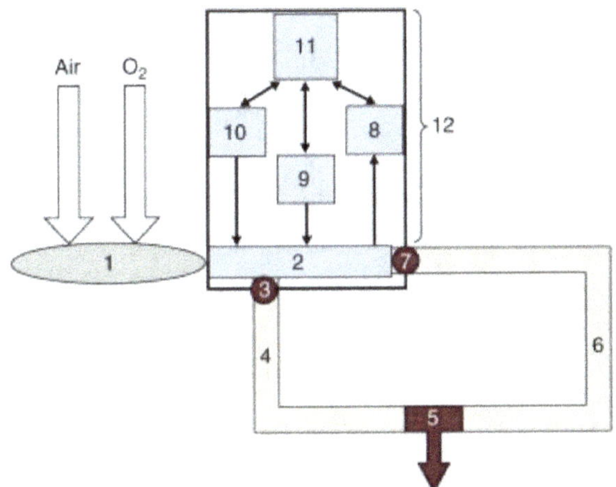

Mechanical ventilation is a sophisticated intervention that requires a deep understanding of the physiological principles underlying its use. This lesson explores the fundamental concepts that govern mechanical ventilation, including respiratory mechanics, gas exchange, and the effects of mechanical ventilation on the cardiovascular system.

Respiratory Mechanics

Respiratory mechanics refers to the physical properties of the respiratory system that influence breathing. Key components of respiratory mechanics include:

- **Compliance:** Compliance is a measure of the lung's ability to expand and contract. It is defined as the change in lung volume per unit change in transpulmonary pressure. High compliance indicates that the lungs are easily distensible, while low compliance suggests stiff or fibrotic lungs.

- **Resistance:** Airway resistance is the opposition to airflow within the respiratory tract. It is influenced by factors such as

"

airway diameter, length, and the viscosity of the gas being inhaled. High resistance can result from conditions such as bronchospasm, mucus plugging, or airway edema.

Gas Exchange

Gas exchange is the process by which oxygen is transferred from the alveoli to the blood, and carbon dioxide is removed from the blood and expelled through the alveoli. Effective gas exchange depends on several factors:

- **Ventilation-perfusion (V/Q) ratio:** The V/Q ratio represents the relationship between alveolar ventilation and pulmonary blood flow. A balanced V/Q ratio is essential for efficient gas exchange. V/Q mismatches, such as those caused by pulmonary embolism or pneumonia, can impair gas exchange and lead to hypoxemia.
- **Diffusion:** The movement of gases across the alveolar-capillary membrane occurs via diffusion. The efficiency of diffusion is influenced by factors such as membrane thickness, surface area, and the partial pressure gradients of oxygen and carbon dioxide.

Effects of Mechanical Ventilation on the Cardiovascular System

Mechanical ventilation can have significant effects on the cardiovascular system. Positive pressure ventilation increases intrathoracic pressure, which can influence venous return, cardiac output, and systemic vascular resistance. Key cardiovascular effects of mechanical ventilation include:

- **Decreased venous return:** Positive pressure ventilation increases intrathoracic pressure, which can reduce venous return to the heart and decrease preload. This effect is more pronounced in hypovolemic patients.
- **Altered cardiac output:** Changes in preload and afterload can influence cardiac output. Mechanical ventilation can

either increase or decrease cardiac output, depending on the patient's volume status and cardiac function.

- **Changes in systemic vascular resistance:** Positive pressure ventilation can lead to vasodilation and decreased systemic vascular resistance, which can further affect cardiac output. Understanding these cardiovascular effects is crucial for managing patients on mechanical ventilation, as it helps optimize hemodynamic status and ensure adequate tissue perfusion.

Lung-Protective Ventilation Strategies

Lung-protective ventilation strategies are designed to minimize ventilator-induced lung injury (VILI) while ensuring adequate gas exchange. These strategies include:

- Low Tidal Volume Ventilation: Using lower tidal volumes (6-8 ml/kg of ideal body weight) to prevent overdistension and reduce the risk of barotrauma and volutrauma.
- Optimal PEEP: Setting positive end-expiratory pressure (PEEP) to maintain alveolar recruitment and prevent atelectasis while avoiding excessive levels that can cause lung injury.
- Limiting Plateau Pressure: Keeping plateau pressures below 30 cm H2O to minimize the risk of alveolar overdistension and lung injury.

Work of Breathing

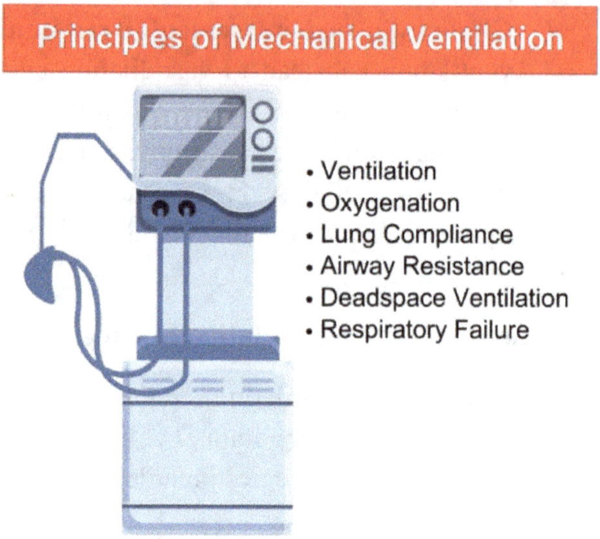

The work of breathing (WOB) refers to the energy expended by respiratory muscles to ventilate the lungs. Mechanical ventilation can reduce the work of breathing by assisting or completely taking over the effort required to inhale and exhale. This is particularly important for patients with respiratory muscle fatigue or failure. Key aspects of WOB include:

- Inspiratory Effort: The effort required to draw air into the lungs. Mechanical ventilation can reduce inspiratory effort by providing positive pressure during inspiration.
- Expiratory Effort is the effort required to expel air from the lungs. In conditions like COPD, where expiratory flow limitation is a concern, mechanical ventilation can help reduce expiratory effort by prolonging expiratory time.

Ventilator-Induced Lung Injury (VILI)

Ventilator-induced lung injury (VILI) is a potential complication of mechanical ventilation that results from the physical forces applied to the lungs during ventilation. VILI can manifest in several ways:

- Barotrauma: Injury caused by high airway pressures, leading to alveolar rupture and air leaks (e.g., pneumothorax, pneumomediastinum).
- Volutrauma: Injury caused by excessive tidal volumes, leading to overdistension and damage to the alveolar-capillary membrane.
- Atelectrauma: Injury caused by repetitive opening and closing of alveoli, leading to shear stress and inflammatory responses.
- Biotrauma: Inflammatory injury resulting from the release of cytokines and other inflammatory mediators in response to mechanical ventilation.

Synchrony and Asynchrony

Patient-ventilator synchrony refers to the coordination between the patient's spontaneous breathing efforts and the ventilator's delivered breaths. Asynchrony can occur when there is a mismatch between the patient's efforts and the ventilator's support, leading to discomfort, increased work breathing, and potential lung injury. Types of asynchrony include:

- Trigger Asynchrony: This occurs when the ventilator fails to detect the patient's inspiratory effort, leading to delayed or missed breaths.
- Flow Asynchrony occurs when the ventilator's flow rate does not match the patient's demand, leading to discomfort and increased breathing work.
- Cycle Asynchrony: Occurs when the ventilator terminates the breath too early or too late relative to the patient's effort.

Understanding and addressing asynchrony is crucial for optimizing patient comfort and ventilator effectiveness.

DISCUSSION QUESTIONS

- What are the most critical parameters to monitor in a mechanically ventilated patient, and how do these parameters inform clinical decisions?
- Discuss the advantages and limitations of using arterial blood gases (ABGs) versus continuous capnography in monitoring ventilated patients.

MODULE THREE

LESSON ONE: MODES OF VENTILATION

Mechanical ventilators offer various modes of ventilation, each designed to meet specific clinical needs and patient conditions. Understanding the different modes of ventilation and their appropriate

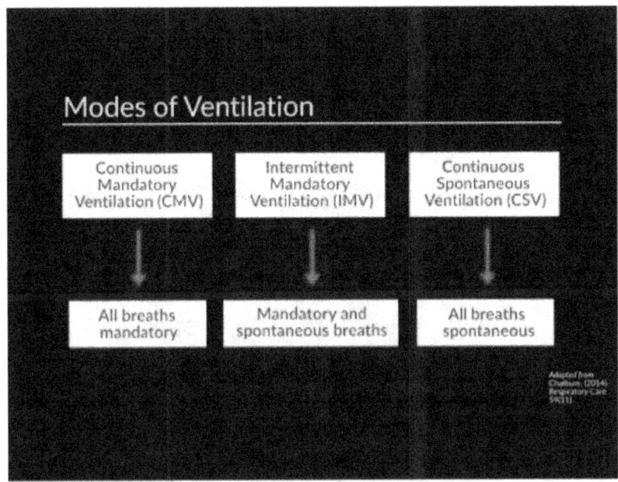

use is crucial for effective mechanical ventilation management. Each mode offers unique advantages and limitations, and selecting the right mode depends on the patient's clinical condition and ventilatory needs.

1. Volume-Controlled Ventilation (VCV)

Volume-controlled ventilation (VCV) is a mode where the ventilator delivers a set tidal volume with each breath. The key features of VCV include:

- Set Parameters: Tidal volume (VT), respiratory rate (RR), and inspiratory flow rate.
- Consistent Tidal Volume: The ventilator delivers a consistent volume for each breath, regardless of changes in airway resistance or lung compliance.
- Pressure Variability: Airway pressures can vary depending on the patient's lung mechanics.

Indications:

- Patients with relatively stable lung mechanics.
- Situations where consistent tidal volume delivery is crucial, such as in ARDS.

Advantages:

- Ensures a predetermined tidal volume is delivered with each breath.
- Simplifies the monitoring of minute ventilation (VE).

Limitations:

- Potential for high airway pressures in patients with poor lung compliance or high airway resistance.
- Risk of volutrauma if tidal volumes are set too high.

2. Pressure-Controlled Ventilation (PCV)

Pressure-controlled ventilation (PCV) is a mode where the ventilator delivers breaths at a set inspiratory pressure. The key features of PCV include:

- Set Parameters: Inspiratory pressure, respiratory rate (RR), and inspiratory time.
- Consistent Pressure: Each breath is delivered at a consistent pressure, resulting in variable tidal volumes depending on lung mechanics.

Indications:

- Patients with variable or poor lung compliance.
- Situations requiring tight control of peak inspiratory pressures, such as in ARDS or acute lung injury.

Advantages:

- Limits peak airway pressures, reducing the risk of barotrauma.
- It can improve oxygenation by allowing longer inspiratory times.

Limitations:

- Tidal volumes can vary, making it challenging to ensure adequate minute ventilation.
- Requires close monitoring and adjustment based on patient response.

3. Assist-Control Ventilation (ACV)

Assist-control ventilation (ACV) is a mode that provides full ventilatory support, with each breath being either patient-initiated or time-triggered. The key features of ACV include:

- Set Parameters: Tidal volume or inspiratory pressure, respiratory rate (RR), and sensitivity.
- Full Support: Every breath is supported by the ventilator, ensuring consistent ventilation.

Indications:

- Patients requiring full respiratory support.
- Acute respiratory failure or during the initial phase of mechanical ventilation.

Advantages:

- Provides consistent and reliable ventilation.
- Reduces the work of breathing for the patient.

Limitations:

- Risk of hyperventilation if the patient has a high respiratory drive.
- Potential for respiratory alkalosis due to excessive ventilation.

4. Synchronized Intermittent Mandatory Ventilation (SIMV)

Synchronized intermittent mandatory ventilation (SIMV) is a mode that combines mandatory breaths with patient-initiated breaths. The key features of SIMV include:

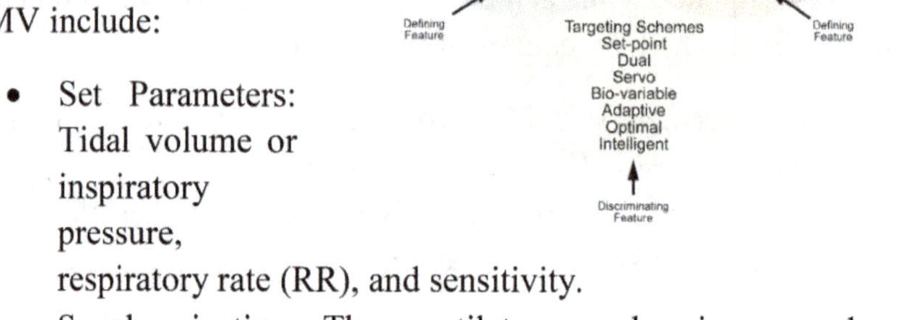

- Set Parameters: Tidal volume or inspiratory pressure, respiratory rate (RR), and sensitivity.
- Synchronization: The ventilator synchronizes mandatory breaths with the patient's spontaneous efforts.

Indications:

- Patients transitioning from full ventilatory support to spontaneous breathing.
- Situations requiring a balance between ventilator support and patient effort.

Advantages:

- Allows for spontaneous breathing, reducing the risk of muscle atrophy.
- Facilitates weaning from mechanical ventilation.

Limitations:

- Potential for asynchrony if the patient's spontaneous breaths are not well synchronized with mandatory breaths.
- Requires careful monitoring to balance support and spontaneous effort.

5. Pressure Support Ventilation (PSV)

Pressure support ventilation (PSV) is a mode where the ventilator provides a preset level of pressure support during spontaneous breaths. The key features of PSV include:

- Set Parameters: Inspiratory pressure support and sensitivity.
- Patient-Triggered: All breaths are patient-initiated and supported by the ventilator.

Indications:

- Patients capable of initiating spontaneous breaths.
- Weaning patients from mechanical ventilation.

Advantages:

- Reduces the work of breathing while allowing spontaneous breathing.
- Improves patient comfort and synchrony.

Limitations:

- Not suitable for patients requiring full ventilatory support.
- Tidal volumes can vary, necessitating close monitoring.

6. Adaptive Support Ventilation (ASV)

Adaptive support ventilation (ASV) is an advanced mode that automatically adjusts ventilator settings based on the patient's respiratory mechanics and effort. The key features of ASV include:

- Adaptive Algorithm: Continuously adjusts tidal volume, respiratory rate, and pressure support to meet the patient's needs.
- Closed-Loop Control: Uses feedback from the patient's breathing to optimize ventilation.

Indications:

- Patients with varying respiratory mechanics.
- Situations requiring automated adjustment of ventilatory support.

Advantages:

- Provides optimal ventilation tailored to the patient's needs.
- Reduces the risk of ventilator-induced lung injury.

Limitations:

- Requires advanced understanding and monitoring of the ventilator's algorithm.
- It may only be suitable for some clinical scenarios.

DISCUSSION QUESTIONS

- Compare and contrast Assist-Control (AC) ventilation and Synchronized Intermittent Mandatory Ventilation (SIMV). What are the advantages and potential drawbacks of each mode in different patient populations?
- Discuss the role of Pressure Support Ventilation (PSV) in the weaning process from mechanical ventilation. How does it aid in transitioning patients from full ventilatory support to spontaneous breathing?

<h1 align="center">MODULE FOUR</h1>

<h2 align="center">LESSON ONE: VENTILATOR SETTINGS</h2>

Ventilator settings are critical parameters that healthcare providers adjust to tailor mechanical ventilation to the patient's specific needs. This lesson provides a detailed exploration of key ventilator settings and how to optimize them for effective respiratory support.

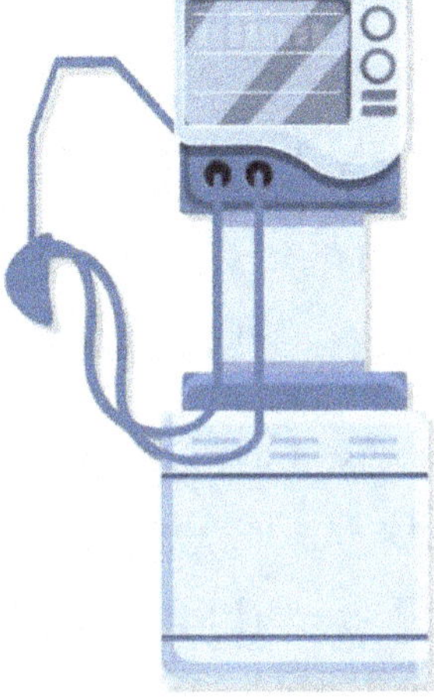

1. Tidal Volume (VT)

Tidal volume (VT) is the volume of air delivered to the lungs with each breath. It is a fundamental setting in mechanical ventilation and is typically set based on the patient's ideal body weight (IBW). The recommended tidal volume is usually 6-8 ml/kg of IBW to minimize the risk of ventilator-induced lung injury.

Key Considerations:

- Low Tidal Volumes: Using lower tidal volumes (4-6 ml/kg IBW) can reduce the risk of volutrauma, especially in patients with ARDS
- High Tidal Volumes: Higher tidal volumes (8-10 ml/kg IBW) may be used in patients without lung injury to ensure adequate ventilation. However, this must be done cautiously to avoid overdistension and barotrauma.

2. Respiratory Rate (RR)

The respiratory rate (RR) is the number of breaths delivered by the ventilator per minute. Adjusting the respiratory rate helps control the patient's minute ventilation (VE), which is the total volume of gas entering the lungs per minute. Minute ventilation is calculated as RR x VT.

Key Considerations:

- Hypoventilation: A low respiratory rate can lead to hypoventilation, which can result in hypercapnia (elevated carbon dioxide levels).
- Hyperventilation: A high respiratory rate can cause hyperventilation, which can lead to hypocapnia (reduced carbon dioxide levels) and respiratory alkalosis.

3. Positive End-Expiratory Pressure (PEEP)

Positive end-expiratory pressure (PEEP) is the pressure maintained in the lungs at the end of exhalation. PEEP helps keep the alveoli open, preventing atelectasis (collapse of alveoli) and improving oxygenation.

Key Considerations:

- Optimal PEEP: Finding the optimal PEEP level involves balancing adequate alveolar recruitment with minimizing overdistension. Too high PEEP can lead to barotrauma and impaired venous return.
- ARDS: In ARDS patients, higher PEEP levels may be required to maintain alveolar recruitment and improve oxygenation.

4. Fraction of Inspired Oxygen (FiO2)

The fraction of inspired oxygen (FiO2) is the concentration of oxygen delivered to the patient. It ranges from 21% (room air) to 100% (pure oxygen).

Key Considerations:

- Oxygen Toxicity: Prolonged exposure to high FiO2 levels can cause oxygen toxicity and lung injury. FiO2 should be titrated to maintain adequate oxygenation (e.g., SpO2 > 92% or PaO2 > 60 mm Hg) while minimizing the risk of toxicity.
- Weaning: Gradually reducing FiO2 is part of the weaning process as the patient's condition improves.

5. Flow Rate

The flow rate is the speed at which the ventilator delivers the gas during the inspiratory phase. It can be adjusted to match the patient's demand and comfort.

Key Considerations:

- High Flow Rates: High flow rates can meet the patient's inspiratory demand but may increase airway resistance and turbulence.
- Low Flow Rates: Low flow rates can improve gas distribution and comfort but may prolong inspiratory time and reduce mean airway pressure.

6. Trigger Sensitivity

Trigger sensitivity determines how easily the ventilator detects the patient's spontaneous breaths. It can be set based on pressure or flow.

Key Considerations:

- Pressure Trigger: A set pressure change initiates a breath. Too sensitive a setting can cause auto-triggering, while too insensitive a setting can increase the work of breathing.
- Flow Trigger: A set change in flow initiates a breath. Flow triggering is often more comfortable for the patient and reduces the work of breathing.

Monitoring and Adjusting Settings

Continuous monitoring and adjustment of ventilator settings are crucial to ensure optimal ventilation and patient safety. Key parameters to monitor include:

- Arterial Blood Gases (ABGs): Regular ABG analysis helps assess the effectiveness of ventilation and oxygenation and guide setting adjustments.
- Ventilator Waveforms: Analyzing waveforms (pressure, volume, and flow) provides insights into patient-ventilator interaction and helps identify issues like asynchrony or air trapping.
- Patient Comfort: Ensuring patient comfort and synchrony with the ventilator is essential. Sedation and analgesia may be necessary for patients experiencing discomfort or anxiety.

Weaning from Mechanical Ventilation

Weaning is the process of gradually reducing ventilatory support as the patient's condition improves. Key strategies for weaning include:

- Spontaneous Breathing Trials (SBTs): SBTs involve periods where the patient breathes spontaneously with minimal support to assess readiness for extubation.
- Gradual Reduction of Support: Gradually reducing pressure support, PEEP, and FiO_2 helps transition the patient to spontaneous breathing.
- Assessing Readiness: Criteria for readiness to wean include stable hemodynamics, adequate oxygenation, and the ability to initiate spontaneous breaths.

DISCUSSION QUESTIONS

- How do changes in Positive End-Expiratory Pressure (PEEP) influence oxygenation and ventilation in patients with ARDS? What are the risks associated with high levels of PEEP?

- What factors should be considered when setting the tidal volume for a patient with acute respiratory distress syndrome (ARDS), and how do these factors impact patient outcomes?

23

Mechanical ventilation can present various challenges, and troubleshooting is a critical skill for healthcare providers. This lesson addresses common issues encountered during mechanical ventilation and provides strategies for effective troubleshooting.

1. High Airway Pressures

High airway pressures can indicate problems with the ventilator circuit or the patient's respiratory system. Common causes include:

- **Airway Obstruction:** Mucus plugs, bronchospasm, or kinking of the endotracheal tube can increase airway resistance and cause high pressures. Suctioning, bronchodilators, and ensuring the tube is patent can resolve this issue.

- **Reduced Lung Compliance**: Conditions like ARDS, pulmonary edema, or pneumothorax can reduce lung compliance and increase pressures. Treating the underlying condition and optimizing ventilator settings can help.

- **Incorrect Ventilator Settings:** High tidal volumes or inappropriate PEEP levels can cause high pressures. Adjusting these settings can reduce pressures and prevent lung injury.

2. Low-Exhaled Tidal Volumes

Low exhaled tidal volumes can compromise ventilation and indicate issues such as:

- **Circuit Leaks:** Leaks in the ventilator circuit, around the endotracheal tube, or in chest tubes can result in low tidal volumes. Checking and securing connections can resolve leaks.
- **Poor Patient Effort:** In spontaneous modes, inadequate patient effort due to sedation, fatigue, or neuromuscular weakness can cause low volumes. Assessing and addressing the underlying cause is essential.
- **Auto-PEEP:** Intrinsic PEEP caused by incomplete exhalation can reduce effective tidal volumes. Increasing expiratory time and reducing respiratory rate can help manage auto-PEEP.

3. Patient-Ventilator Asynchrony

Asynchrony between the patient and the ventilator can lead to discomfort, increased work of breathing, and compromised ventilation. Common types of asynchrony include:

- Trigger Asynchrony: Difficulty in initiating breaths due to inappropriate trigger sensitivity. Adjusting sensitivity settings or switching to flow triggering can improve synchrony.
- Flow Asynchrony: Mismatch between the ventilator's flow rate and the patient's demand. Adjusting inspiratory flow rates or switching to pressure support modes can help.
- Cycle Asynchrony: Premature or delayed termination of breaths. Adjusting inspiratory time or switching to modes that allow better synchrony can resolve this issue.

4. Hypoxemia

Hypoxemia during mechanical ventilation can result from various factors, including:

- V/Q Mismatch: Ventilation-perfusion mismatches can be caused by conditions like atelectasis, pneumonia, or pulmonary embolism. Treating the underlying condition and optimizing PEEP and FiO2 can improve oxygenation.
- Shunt: Intrapulmonary shunting due to severe lung pathology. Strategies like recruitment manoeuvres, prone positioning, and high PEEP can help.
- Low FiO2: Inadequate oxygen delivery due to low FiO2 settings. Increasing FiO2 while monitoring for oxygen toxicity is crucial.

5. Hypercapnia

Hypercapnia, or elevated carbon dioxide levels, can occur due to:

- Hypoventilation: Inadequate minute ventilation due to low tidal volumes or respiratory rate. Increasing ventilatory support can correct hypercapnia.
- Increased Dead Space: Conditions like pulmonary embolism or severe emphysema can increase dead space ventilation. Addressing the underlying cause and optimizing ventilation can help.
- CO2 Rebreathing: Rebreathing of exhaled CO2 due to circuit malfunction or inadequate expiratory time. Ensuring proper circuit function and adjusting expiratory time can prevent rebreathing.

6. Alarms and Alerts

Ventilators are equipped with alarms to alert healthcare providers to potential issues. Common alarms include:

- High Pressure Alarm: Indicates high airway pressures. Assessing and addressing the cause of high pressures is essential.

- Low Tidal Volume Alarm: This alarm indicates inadequate tidal volumes. It can result from leaks, poor patient effort, or auto-PEEP. It is necessary to check for circuit integrity, patient condition, and ventilator settings.
- High Respiratory Rate Alarm: This alarm indicates rapid breathing, which can be due to pain, anxiety, or respiratory distress. Assessing and addressing the underlying cause, providing sedation, or adjusting ventilator settings can help.
- Apnea Alarm: Indicates the absence of spontaneous breaths in modes requiring patient effort. Ensuring proper ventilator settings and addressing causes like sedation or respiratory muscle fatigue is crucial.

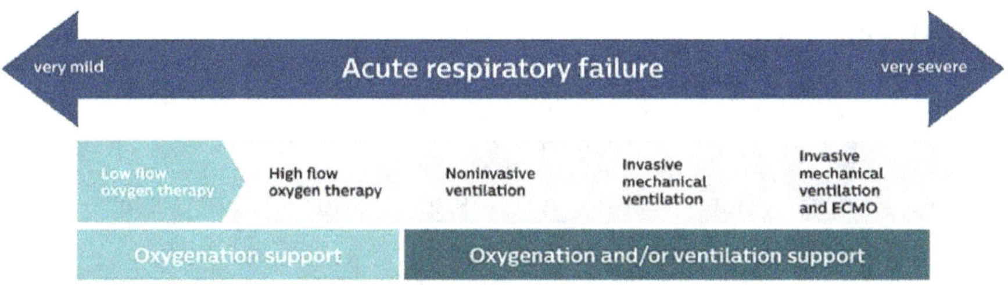

Managing Circuit and Equipment Issues

Proper maintenance and troubleshooting of the ventilator circuit and equipment are essential to ensure effective ventilation.

1. Circuit Leaks and Disconnections:
   - Regularly check all connections in the ventilator circuit to ensure they are secure.
   - Inspect the endotracheal tube cuff for leaks and ensure proper inflation.
   - Replace any damaged or worn-out components promptly.
2. **Condensation in the Circuit:**
   - Condensation can accumulate in the ventilator circuit, particularly in humidified systems.
   - Regularly drain condensation from the circuit to prevent it from interfering with ventilation.

- Use heated circuits or water traps to minimize condensation build-up.

3. **Ventilator Performance and Functionality:**
   - Regularly perform ventilator checks and calibrations as recommended by the manufacturer.
   - Ensure that the ventilator is functioning correctly and delivering the set parameters.
   - Keep backup equipment available in case of ventilator malfunction.

4. **Documentation and Communication**

Accurate documentation and effective communication are critical for managing mechanical ventilation.

Documentation:

- Document ventilator settings, patient parameters, and any changes made to the settings.
- Record ABG results, vital signs, and patient assessments regularly.
- Note any issues encountered and the actions taken to address them.

Communication:

- Ensure clear communication between the healthcare team members regarding the patient's ventilatory status and any changes in settings.
- Use standardized protocols and handoff tools to ensure consistency in patient care.
- Involve respiratory therapists, nurses, and physicians in collaborative decision-making for ventilator management.

Case Studies and Scenarios

Discussing real-life case studies and scenarios can enhance understanding and provide practical insights into troubleshooting mechanical ventilation issues.

Case Study 1: ARDS Management

- A patient with ARDS presents with high airway pressures and refractory hypoxemia.
- Strategies include adjusting the tidal volume to 6 ml/kg IBW, increasing PEEP, and considering prone positioning.
- Regular monitoring of ABGs and patient response to interventions guides further adjustments.

Case Study 2: COPD Exacerbation

- A patient with COPD exacerbation requires mechanical ventilation due to hypercapnic respiratory failure.
- Initial settings include low tidal volumes and longer expiratory times to prevent air trapping.
- Bronchodilators and steroids are administered to address underlying bronchospasm.

Scenario: Ventilator Malfunction

- During a night shift, a ventilator malfunctions and triggers multiple alarms.
- The healthcare team quickly assesses the patient's status and switches to a backup ventilator.
- Detailed documentation of the incident and maintenance checks on the malfunctioning ventilator are performed.

Effective troubleshooting of common issues in mechanical ventilation requires a comprehensive understanding of ventilator settings, patient-ventilator interaction, and equipment maintenance. By systematically addressing these challenges and maintaining clear documentation and communication, healthcare providers can ensure optimal ventilatory support and patient outcomes.

DISCUSSION QUESTIONS

- What are the potential causes of high-pressure alarms in mechanical ventilation, and how should they be systematically investigated and resolved?
- Describe the steps you would take to identify and correct the cause of a low tidal volume alarm in a patient receiving mechanical ventilation.

MODULE SIX

LESSON ONE: PROVIDING OPTIMAL SUPPORT TO PATIENTS WITH RESPIRATORY FAILURE

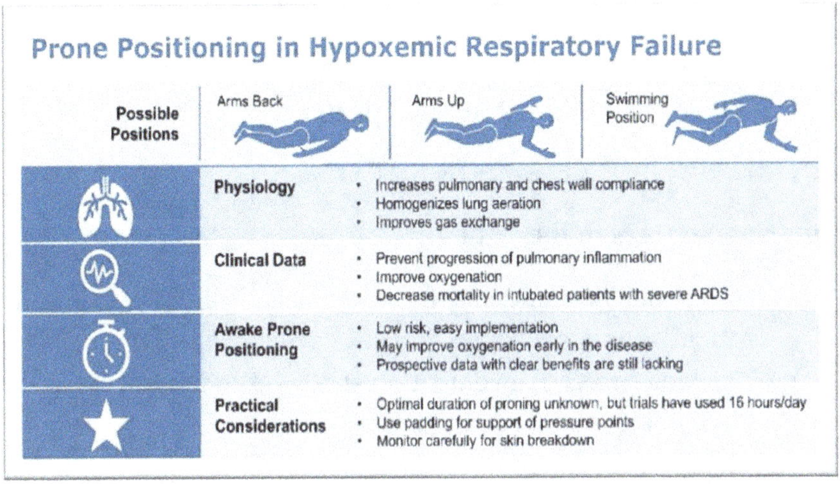

Prone Positioning in Hypoxemic Respiratory Failure

Possible Positions	Arms Back	Arms Up	Swimming Position

Physiology	• Increases pulmonary and chest wall compliance • Homogenizes lung aeration • Improves gas exchange
Clinical Data	• Prevent progression of pulmonary inflammation • Improve oxygenation • Decrease mortality in intubated patients with severe ARDS
Awake Prone Positioning	• Low risk, easy implementation • May improve oxygenation early in the disease • Prospective data with clear benefits are still lacking
Practical Considerations	• Optimal duration of proning unknown, but trials have used 16 hours/day • Use padding for support of pressure points • Monitor carefully for skin breakdown

Providing optimal support to patients with respiratory failure involves a combination of appropriate ventilator settings, continuous monitoring, and individualized patient care. Providing optimal support to patients with respiratory failure involves a combination of individualized ventilator settings, continuous monitoring, and a multidisciplinary approach. By tailoring care to the specific needs of each patient and involving the healthcare team and family, providers can improve outcomes and enhance the quality of care for patients with respiratory failure.

INITIAL ASSESSMENT AND STABILIZATION

Clinical Assessment:

- Conduct a thorough clinical assessment, including patient history, physical examination, and evaluation of respiratory status.

- Identify the underlying cause of respiratory failure (e.g., ARDS, COPD exacerbation, pneumonia) to guide treatment.

Stabilization:

- Ensure airway patency and secure the endotracheal tube.
- Initiate mechanical ventilation with appropriate settings based on the patient's condition.
- Monitor vital signs, oxygenation, and ventilation closely during the initial stabilization phase.

OPTIMIZING VENTILATOR SETTINGS

Tailoring Settings to the Patient:

- Adjust tidal volume, respiratory rate, and PEEP based on the patient's lung mechanics and gas exchange needs.
- Use lung-protective ventilation strategies to minimize the risk of ventilator-induced lung injury.

Monitoring and Adjusting:

- Continuously monitor ABGs, ventilator waveforms, and patient comfort.
- Adjust ventilator settings as needed to maintain optimal oxygenation and ventilation while minimizing adverse effects.

Managing Specific Conditions

1. **ARDS:**
   - To improve oxygenation and reduce lung injury, use low tidal volumes (4-6 ml/kg IBW) and higher PEEP levels.
   - Consider adjunctive therapies such as prone positioning and neuromuscular blockade in severe cases.
2. **COPD:**
   - Use lower tidal volumes and prolonged expiratory times to prevent air trapping and hyperinflation.
   - Administer bronchodilators and steroids to manage airway obstruction and inflammation.

Pneumonia:

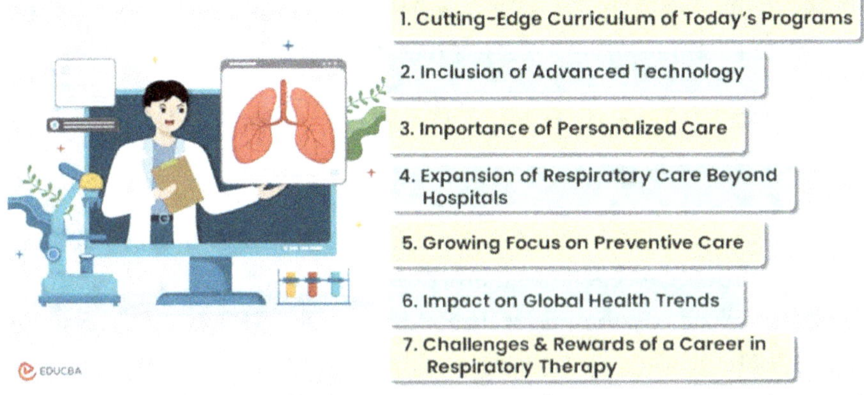

- Optimize ventilation to ensure adequate oxygenation and support gas exchange.
- Administer appropriate antibiotics and supportive care to treat the underlying infection.

Heart Failure:

- Use ventilator settings that minimize cardiac workload and optimize oxygen delivery.
- Administer diuretics and other medications to manage fluid balance and improve cardiac function.

SEDATION AND ANALGESIA

Assessing Sedation Needs:

- Assess the patient's level of sedation regularly using standardized scales (e.g., Richmond Agitation-Sedation Scale, RASS).
- Adjust sedation and analgesia to ensure patient comfort and reduce anxiety while avoiding over-sedation.

Sedation Strategies:

- Use a combination of medications (e.g., benzodiazepines, opioids, propofol) to achieve the desired level of sedation.
- Consider daily sedation interruptions or spontaneous awakening trials to assess readiness for weaning.

WEANING AND EXTUBATION

Criteria for Weaning:

- Evaluate readiness for weaning based on clinical stability, adequate oxygenation, and spontaneous breathing capability.
- Conduct spontaneous breathing trials (SBTs) to assess the patient's ability to breathe without ventilatory support.

Weaning Process:

- Gradually reduce ventilatory support, including pressure support and PEEP, while monitoring patient response.
- Provide adequate respiratory muscle training and support to facilitate successful weaning.

Extubation:

- Ensure the patient meets extubation criteria, including adequate airway protection, a strong cough, and minimal secretions.
- Monitor closely for signs of respiratory distress or failure post-extubation and provide appropriate support if needed.

MULTIDISCIPLINARY APPROACH

Collaboration:

- Foster collaboration among the healthcare team, including physicians, nurses, respiratory therapists, and other specialists.
- Implement multidisciplinary rounds and discussions to ensure comprehensive patient care and effective decision-making.

Family Involvement:

- Involve the patient's family in the care plan, providing education and support to help them understand the patient's condition and treatment.
- Address family concerns and preferences, ensuring they are informed and involved in care decisions.

Case Studies and Practical Applications

Case Study 1: ARDS Management:

- A 45-year-old patient with ARDS secondary to sepsis requires mechanical ventilation.
- Initial settings include low tidal volumes, higher PEEP, and prone positioning.
- Continuous monitoring and adjustments based on ABGs and clinical response guide the management.

Case Study 2: COPD Exacerbation:

- A 60-year-old patient with COPD exacerbation presents with respiratory acidosis and hypercapnia.
- Ventilator settings include low tidal volumes, prolonged expiratory time, and bronchodilator therapy.
- Gradual reduction of support and weaning trials lead to successful extubation.

DISCUSSION QUESTIONS

- How can sedation and analgesia be optimized to balance patient comfort and effective ventilatory support without leading to over-sedation?
- Discuss the criteria and process for weaning a patient from mechanical ventilation. What factors influence the timing and success of extubation?

MODULE SEVEN

LESSON ONE: LATEST ADVANCEMENTS IN RESPIRATORY CARE

1. High-Frequency Oscillatory Ventilation (HFOV)

High-frequency oscillatory ventilation (HFOV) is a mode of ventilation that delivers very small tidal volumes at very high frequencies (up to 900 breaths per minute). It is used primarily in patients

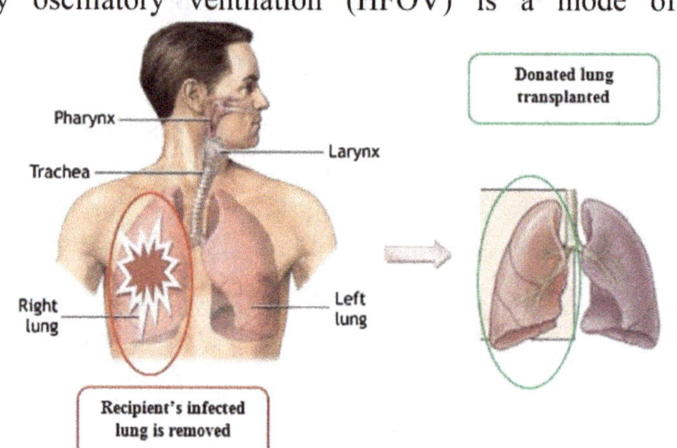

with severe ARDS who are not responding to conventional ventilation strategies.

Mechanism:

- HFOV maintains constant mean airway pressure to keep alveoli open and improve oxygenation.
- The small tidal volumes minimize the risk of ventilator-induced lung injury (VILI).

Indications:

- Severe ARDS with refractory hypoxemia.
- Patients failing conventional lung-protective ventilation strategies.

Advantages:

- Reduces the risk of VILI by minimizing volutrauma and barotrauma.
- Provides effective oxygenation and ventilation in severe lung injury.

Limitations:

- Requires specialized equipment and expertise.
- Potential for hemodynamic instability due to high mean airway pressures.

2. Extracorporeal Membrane Oxygenation (ECMO)

Extracorporeal membrane oxygenation (ECMO) is an advanced therapy that provides cardiac and respiratory support to patients with severe respiratory or cardiac failure. ECMO involves circulating the patient's blood through an external oxygenator.

Types of ECMO:

- Veno-Venous (VV) ECMO: Provides respiratory support for severe lung failure.
- Veno-Arterial (VA) ECMO: Provides both cardiac and respiratory support for patients with combined cardiac and respiratory failure.

Indications:

- Severe ARDS is unresponsive to conventional therapies.
- Cardiogenic shock is refractory to medical management.
- Bridge to lung transplant or recovery in select cases.

Advantages:

- Provides oxygenation and CO_2 removal independent of lung function.
- Allows time for lung recovery or transplantation in severe respiratory failure.

Limitations:

- Requires specialized equipment and expertise.
- Associated with complications such as bleeding, infection, and thrombosis.

3. Airway Pressure Release Ventilation (APRV)

Airway pressure release ventilation (APRV) is a mode of ventilation that provides continuous positive airway pressure (CPAP) with brief releases to allow for spontaneous breathing. APRV is often used in patients with ARDS to improve oxygenation and minimize ventilator-induced lung injury.

Mechanism:

- APRV maintains a high level of CPAP throughout the respiratory cycle, promoting alveolar recruitment and oxygenation.
- Brief releases of pressure allow for spontaneous breathing and CO_2 removal.

Indications:

- Moderate to severe ARDS with refractory hypoxemia.
- Patients requiring lung-protective ventilation strategies.

Advantages:

- Improves oxygenation and CO_2 clearance.
- Minimizes barotrauma and volutrauma associated with traditional ventilation.

Limitations:

- Requires close monitoring of patient response and adjustment of settings.
- It may increase patient discomfort and work of breathing during spontaneous breaths.

Prone Positioning

Prone positioning involves placing the patient in a prone (face-down) position to improve oxygenation and ventilation in patients with ARDS. Prone positioning redistributes ventilation to dependent lung regions, improving ventilation-perfusion matching and reducing ventilator-induced lung injury.

Mechanism:

- Prone positioning improves oxygenation by optimizing lung recruitment and reducing alveolar overdistension.
- It helps alleviate dorsal lung compression and improves ventilation to previously dependent regions.

Indications:

- Severe ARDS with refractory hypoxemia.
- Patients failing conventional ventilation strategies.

Advantages:

- Improves oxygenation and reduces mortality in severe ARDS.
- Enhances lung recruitment and decreases the risk of ventilator-induced lung injury.

Limitations:

- Requires coordination and positioning expertise from the healthcare team.
- Potential for pressure-related injuries and complications associated with pruning manoeuvres.

4. Neuromuscular Blockade

Neuromuscular blockade involves the administration of pharmacological agents to temporarily paralyze skeletal muscles, including the respiratory muscles. It is used in patients with severe respiratory failure to optimize ventilator synchrony, reduce oxygen consumption, and facilitate lung-protective ventilation.

Indications:

- Severe ARDS with refractory hypoxemia and asynchrony.
- Patients requiring deep sedation and ventilator management.

Advantages:

- Improves patient-ventilator synchrony and reduces the risk of barotrauma.
- Allows for lung-protective ventilation strategies and optimization of gas exchange.

Limitations:

- Associated with risks of prolonged paralysis, including muscle weakness and critical illness myopathy.

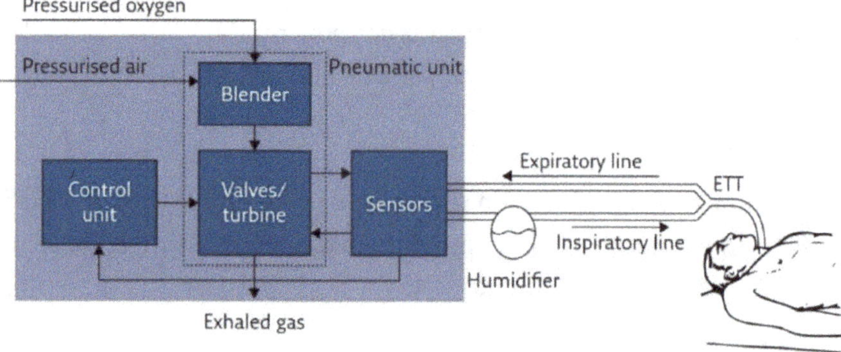

- Requires careful monitoring and titration to prevent over-sedation and complications.

ADJUNCTIVE THERAPIES

Adjunctive therapies, in addition to advanced ventilation modes, play a crucial role in optimizing outcomes in patients with respiratory failure.

Extracorporeal CO2 Removal (ECCO2R):

- ECCO2R removes CO2 from the blood using an extracorporeal circuit, allowing for lung-protective ventilation strategies and preventing respiratory acidosis.

Inhaled Pulmonary Vasodilators:

- Inhaled pulmonary vasodilators such as nitric oxide (NO) or prostacyclin can improve oxygenation by reducing pulmonary vascular resistance and improving blood flow to ventilated lung regions.

Recruitment Maneuvers:

- Recruitment manoeuvres involve transient increases in airway pressure to open collapsed alveoli and improve lung compliance, facilitating oxygenation and ventilation.

Fluid Management:

- Optimal fluid management aims to achieve euvolemia and prevent volume overload, which can exacerbate respiratory failure and impair gas exchange.

EMERGING TECHNOLOGIES

Advancements in technology continue to drive innovation in mechanical ventilation, with several emerging technologies showing promise in improving patient outcomes.

Artificial Intelligence (AI) in Ventilator Management:

- AI algorithms can analyze patient data, predict clinical deterioration, and optimize ventilator settings in real-time, enhancing patient safety and outcomes.

Lung-Protective Ventilation Strategies:

- Novel ventilation strategies, including personalized ventilation and adaptive control algorithms, aim to individualize ventilator settings and minimize ventilator-induced lung injury.

Extracorporeal Lung Assist Devices:

Extracorporeal lung assist devices, such as the Hemolung Respiratory Assist System (RAS), provide partial respiratory support by removing

CO2 and delivering oxygen directly to the blood, allowing for lung-protective ventilation.

- Non-Invasive Ventilation (NIV) Advances:

Advances in non-invasive ventilation techniques, including high-flow nasal cannula (HFNC) therapy and helmet ventilation, offer alternatives to invasive mechanical ventilation in selected patients with respiratory failure.

DISCUSSION QUESTIONS

- In what clinical situations might High-Frequency Oscillatory Ventilation (HFOV) be preferred over conventional ventilation strategies, and what are the key considerations for its use?
- Evaluate the potential benefits and risks of using Extracorporeal Membrane Oxygenation (ECMO) in patients with severe ARDS. How does ECMO complement or replace traditional ventilation strategies?

MODULE EIGHT

LESSON ONE: FUTURE DIRECTIONS IN MECHANICAL VENTILATION

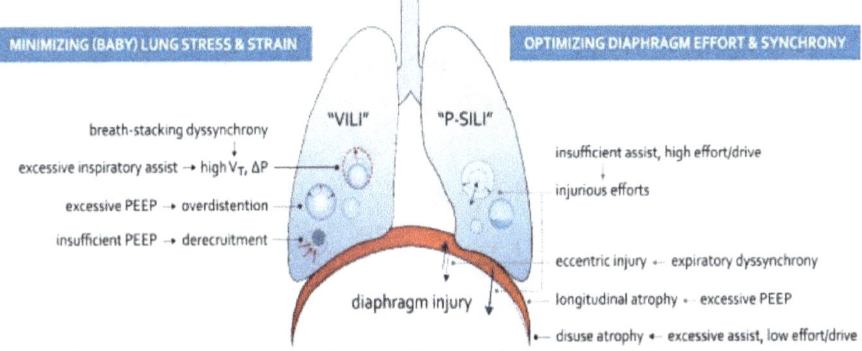

The future of mechanical ventilation holds exciting possibilities, driven by advancements in technology, personalized medicine, and a deeper understanding of respiratory physiology. This lesson explores potential future directions in mechanical ventilation and their implications for patient care and outcomes.

Precision Ventilation

Precision ventilation involves tailoring ventilator settings and strategies to individual patient characteristics, including lung mechanics, gas exchange parameters, and response to therapy. By leveraging data analytics, artificial intelligence, and machine learning algorithms, precision ventilation aims to optimize respiratory support and minimize complications.

Key Components:

- Patient Phenotyping: Identifying patient-specific phenotypes based on clinical, physiological, and genetic factors to guide ventilator management.
- Predictive Modeling: Developing predictive models to anticipate patient responses to different ventilation strategies and interventions.

- Closed-Loop Control: Implementing closed-loop control systems that continuously adapt ventilator settings based on real-time patient data and feedback.

Potential Benefits:

- Improved Outcomes: Personalized ventilation approaches have the potential to improve patient outcomes by minimizing ventilator-induced lung injury, optimizing gas exchange, and reducing complications.
- Enhanced Efficiency: Precision ventilation algorithms can streamline ventilator management by automating decision-making processes and reducing the burden on healthcare providers.
- Reduced Costs: By tailoring ventilation strategies to individual patient needs and responses, precision ventilation may lead to more efficient resource utilization and reduced healthcare costs.

Telemedicine and Remote Monitoring

Telemedicine and remote monitoring technologies enable healthcare providers to monitor ventilated patients remotely, facilitate virtual consultations, and deliver timely interventions. These technologies hold promise for extending critical care expertise to underserved areas, improving access to specialized care, and enhancing patient outcomes.

Applications:

- Remote Monitoring: Continuous monitoring of ventilator parameters, vital signs, and clinical status using wearable devices, remote sensors, and telecommunication platforms.
- Teleconsultation: Virtual consultations between remote intensivists, respiratory therapists, and bedside clinicians to review patient data, discuss management strategies, and provide guidance.

- Tele-ICU: Integration of telemedicine technologies into ICU settings to supplement onsite care with remote monitoring, decision support, and telepresence capabilities.

Benefits:

- Timely Intervention: Remote monitoring allows for early detection of clinical deterioration, enabling prompt interventions and preventing adverse events.
- Access to Expertise: Teleconsultation and tele-ICU services connect bedside providers with critical care specialists, facilitating collaborative decision-making and knowledge exchange.
- Continuity of Care: Telemedicine technologies support seamless transitions of care between different healthcare settings, ensuring consistent monitoring and management of ventilated patients.

BIOMARKERS AND PRECISION MEDICINE

Biomarkers play a crucial role in predicting patient outcomes, guiding treatment decisions, and monitoring response to therapy in mechanical ventilation. As our understanding of respiratory biomarkers expands, precision medicine approaches can tailor ventilation strategies to individual patient profiles, optimizing efficacy and minimizing risks.

Key Biomarkers:

- Inflammatory Markers: Biomarkers of inflammation, such as cytokines, chemokines, and inflammatory cells, provide insights into the underlying pathophysiology of lung injury and response to treatment.
- Lung Injury Biomarkers: Biomarkers of lung injury, including surfactant proteins, lung epithelial markers, and markers of endothelial dysfunction, help assess the severity of lung damage and guide ventilator management.

- Genetic Markers: Genetic variants associated with susceptibility to lung injury, response to mechanical ventilation, and pharmacogenomic factors influence individual patient responses and outcomes.

Clinical Applications:

- Risk Stratification: Biomarkers help identify patients at higher risk of developing ventilator-associated complications, such as ARDS, ventilator-induced lung injury, and respiratory failure.
- Treatment Selection: Biomarker-guided approaches inform the selection of ventilation strategies, adjunctive therapies, and targeted interventions tailored to individual patient profiles and disease trajectories.
- Prognostication: Biomarkers serve as prognostic indicators of clinical outcomes, including mortality, ventilator liberation, and long-term sequelae, guiding decision-making and end-of-life discussions.

Challenges and Opportunities:

- Standardization: Standardizing biomarker assays, interpretation criteria, and clinical thresholds is essential for ensuring consistency and reproducibility across different healthcare settings.
- Integration: Integrating biomarker data into clinical decision support systems and electronic health records facilitates real-time monitoring, data-driven decision-making, and personalized ventilation algorithms.

REGENERATIVE THERAPIES AND TISSUE ENGINEERING

Regenerative therapies and tissue engineering approaches hold promise for restoring lung function, repairing injured tissues, and promoting lung regeneration in patients with respiratory failure. By harnessing stem cells, biomaterials, and tissue engineering techniques, these innovative strategies aim to address the underlying causes of lung injury and enhance recovery.

Emerging Approaches:

- Stem Cell Therapy: The administration of stem cells, including mesenchymal stem cells, endothelial progenitor cells, and lung progenitor cells, has the potential to reduce inflammation, promote tissue repair, and modulate immune responses in acute and chronic lung injury.
- Biomimetic Scaffolds: Biomaterial-based scaffolds mimic the extracellular matrix and provide structural support for cell growth, differentiation, and tissue regeneration, enabling the engineering of functional lung tissues and organoids.
- Gene Editing: Gene editing technologies, such as CRISPR-Cas9, offer precise tools for modifying genetic pathways involved in lung disease, repairing defective genes, and enhancing therapeutic efficacy in respiratory failure.

Clinical Translation:

- Preclinical Studies: Preclinical research in animal models of lung injury and human lung organoids demonstrates the feasibility and efficacy of regenerative therapies in improving lung function, reducing fibrosis, and enhancing recovery.
- Clinical Trials: Clinical trials evaluating the safety, feasibility, and efficacy of regenerative therapies in patients with ARDS, COPD, pulmonary fibrosis, and other respiratory conditions are underway, with promising preliminary results.

Challenges and Considerations:

- Safety: Ensuring the safety and tolerability of regenerative therapies, minimizing off-target effects, and mitigating risks of tumorigenesis and immune rejection are paramount considerations in clinical translation.
- Efficacy: Optimizing the delivery, dosing, and timing of regenerative therapies to maximize efficacy, enhance

engraftment, and promote long-term tissue repair poses challenges in clinical practice.

- Ethical and Regulatory Frameworks: Addressing ethical, legal, and regulatory considerations surrounding the use of stem cells, gene editing, and tissue engineering in clinical research and patient care is essential for ensuring patient safety, informed consent, and equitable access.

DISCUSSION QUESTIONS

- How might precision ventilation, using artificial intelligence and machine learning, change the future landscape of mechanical ventilation? Discuss potential benefits and challenges.
- What are the ethical and regulatory considerations surrounding the use of regenerative therapies and tissue engineering in treating respiratory failure? How should these considerations guide future research and clinical practice?

CONCLUSION

Mechanical ventilation is a cornerstone of critical care medicine, providing essential respiratory support to patients with a wide range of conditions, from acute respiratory distress syndrome (ARDS) to chronic obstructive pulmonary disease (COPD). This comprehensive guide has explored the fundamental principles, advanced modes, and emerging technologies in mechanical ventilation, offering a detailed framework for healthcare providers to optimize patient care.

Understanding the basics of mechanical ventilation, including the physiology of breathing and the technical aspects of ventilators, forms the foundation for effective respiratory support. By mastering different ventilation modes and settings, clinicians can tailor their approach to meet the specific needs of each patient, ensuring adequate oxygenation and ventilation while minimizing the risks of ventilator-induced lung injury.

Monitoring and assessing patients on mechanical ventilation is crucial for timely interventions and adjustments. Continuous vigilance, coupled with advanced monitoring tools, allows for the early detection of issues and the implementation of corrective measures, ultimately improving patient outcomes.

Mechanical ventilation is both an art and a science, requiring a deep understanding of respiratory physiology, technical proficiency, and compassionate patient care. By embracing innovation and striving for excellence, healthcare providers can navigate the complexities of mechanical ventilation and deliver optimal support to those in need.

REFERENCES

- Bittner, E. A., Schmidt, U. H., & George, E. (2016). *Ventilator Modes and Settings. Respiratory Care.*

- Brochard, L., Slutsky, A., & Pesenti, A. (2017). *Mechanical Ventilation to Minimize Progression of Lung Injury in Acute Respiratory Failure. American Journal of Respiratory and Critical Care Medicine.*

- Burns, K. E. A., Lellouche, F., & Lessard, M. R. (2013). *Weaning from Mechanical Ventilation. Clinics in Chest Medicine.*

- Chiumello, D., Brochard, L., Marini, J. J., Slutsky, A. S., & Ranieri, V. M. (2017). *Respiratory Support in Patients with Acute Respiratory Distress Syndrome: An Official American Thoracic Society Clinical Practice Guideline. American Journal of Respiratory and Critical Care Medicine.*

- Fan, E., Beitler, J. R., Brochard, L., Calfee, C. S., & Ferguson, N. D. (2020). *COVID-19-associated Acute Respiratory Distress Syndrome: Is a Different Approach to Management Warranted? The Lancet Respiratory Medicine.*

- Fan, E., Del Sorbo, L., Goligher, E. C., Hodgson, C. L., & Munshi, L. (2017). *An Official American Thoracic Society/European Society of Intensive Care Medicine/Society of Critical Care Medicine Clinical Practice Guideline: Mechanical Ventilation in Adult Patients with Acute Respiratory Distress Syndrome. American Journal of Respiratory and Critical Care Medicine.*